BLOOD SACRIFICE

Center Working Papers are works-in-progress,
or edited texts of interviews, lectures and
symposia presented by
the Center for Studies in American Culture,
a unit of the University at Buffalo,
State University of New York.

For Allee,
love,
Diane
20 December 2003

BLOOD
SACRIFICE

BY DIANE CHRISTIAN

Center Working Papers

This material previously appeared in *CounterPunch* and *Buffalo Report*.

ISBN 0-931627-08-7

CENTER FOR STUDIES IN AMERICAN CULTURE
610 Capen Hall
University at Buffalo
Buffalo, New York 14209
csac@buffalo.edu
http://www.centerworkingpapers.com

Contents

License to kill: the problem with religious definitions of evil

The recently released tape of Osama Bin Laden played on the Arab Al-Jezeera network has been identified by the U.S. government as authentic. It has also been branded inauthentic by some Swiss tape experts and by some Islamic scholars who say the citations are wrong for bin Laden's orthodox style. People suspicious of U.S. government manipulation think the tape appeared when it did to prod passage of the Homeland Security Act.

I'd like to consider it as authentic for purposes of moral analysis. It is consistent with earlier statements by bin Laden and voices his same religious justifications.

What is said? Osama bin Laden, or the person pretending to be him, speaks as 'the slave of God' to the peoples allied with the unjust government of the United States. He argues that Arab peoples have been brutalized and mistreated by the Americans, who deserve to die for this cruelty.

1

The speaker prays piously to his god to support and defend him and all good Muslims in their war against the infidels. The Islamic society will, he says, with God's help, "fight you with its children, who have promised God to continue to fight hard to reach justice and stop injustice as long as they live." This war, he says, is spreading ㄱ.d increasingly successful. The attacks on New York and Washington have been followed by attacks in Tunis, Karachi, Yemen, Failaka, Bali and Moscow by the sons of Islam who are fulfilling the orders of their god and their prophet.

This is the same logic and rhetoric of the Crusades. There God protected his Christian people as they sought to wrest the holy lands from the perfidious hands of the Muslim infidel.

The problem with a religious license to kill is that it's unarguable. If people are inspired and believe their cause righteous they will be martyrs among the believers, even if branded fanatics or malefactors by the enemy. Bin Laden's religious appeal is as real as Joan of Arc's.

And bin Laden's second appeal is also familiar – his people have suffered. Leaders of many stripes appeal to national humiliation, persecution or disgrace as justification for acts of revenge or reprisal. Hitler constantly intoned Germany's humiliation in World War I. Milosevic spoke of Serbian defeats centuries past as rationale for Serbian retaliation. The Israeli cry of 'never again' summons the Holocaust as justification of self-defense warfare and aggression.

Those who believe themselves embattled, aggrieved or entitled to conquer error, easily assume the mantle of just war. Bin Laden calls Bush the pharaoh of today (some experts say he would never mix religious metaphor in this way) and says Bush and Israel, the ally of America, kill children and the elderly and destroy houses. He warns other nations to avoid this criminal gang. But mostly he says that they and those who aid them shall be righteously killed in retribution for the killing they have done. "As you kill, you will be killed. As you bomb you will be bombed and wait for the bad." He presents himself not as a terrorist but as a righteous avenger following god's will.

We citizens of the United States embrace tolerance as a national value and separate church and state; we constitutionally refuse to establish religion. But many American Christian leaders preach openly against Muslims, and many Christian leaders who preach for strong military support of Israel do so in anticipation of a time when Israel is destroyed or converted and the Christian Messiah comes to Jerusalem in glory. If bin Laden says we are decadent and corrupt and should be destroyed, and we say he is evil and fanatical and should be destroyed, what do the utterances mean except that we're justified in killing each other? For us, our gods become the ratifiers of our goodness; for our opponents, they are the rationalization of our evil.

The version of Christianity that I like refuses violence. I'm for the Christ who won't smite his oppressors, who says if someone strikes you turn the other cheek, who says to love your enemy and do good to them that hate you. Some might quarrel that the same Christ comes finally in Christian judgment to separate the good and the evil – inviting the former to eternal glory and banishing the latter to eternal perdition. Eternal violence, some might say, makes up for temporal pacifism.

Maybe so, but we should note that we're in time and we're not god. The principle of being good or bad for the Christ I like is doing good to your fellow human being – feeding the hungry, clothing the naked, sheltering the homeless, visiting the imprisoned. To do this to the least is to do it to God says Christ.

But can I impose this belief on you, can I kill you if you don't accept it or convert? Christianity sometimes did. It also murdered in revenge. The root of Christian anti-Semitism and persecution is blaming the Jews for killing Christ – a position officially disowned only recently.

I think the only acceptable moral position is to give everybody the liberty to choose their god and good, or their non-god good and insist that all be allowed and none licensed.

Most Americans feel comfortably superior to nations which issue death sentences for blasphemy and stone adulterous women. As the world becomes smaller, we need to think about values we can honestly stand for and support. The value of human life is primary and supercedes all others. We should act for that good and not imitate the evil we seek to abolish. The real religious truth is that we are the evil we hate if we mirror it. There is a difference between good and evil, between life and death, between killing or not. Those who murdered and fomented murder on September 11, 2001 are murderers, as are those who murder in revenge.

To piously proclaim worship and submission to god's will does not make anyone god or his prophet. There are no legitimate religious licenses to kill.

warriors

when they mount
the high moral horses
they're about
to trample you

The Morality of Violence

The dilemma Bush and Blair and Powell set for us is: the bottom line is violence. If the tyrant won't disarm and will use diplomacy to flaunt and manipulate, the only recourse is to take him out – 'regime change' in political speech. They say the only thing that has brought even token cooperation from Saddam Hussein is massive arms buildup at his borders and time is up for talking. This is *The Art of War, Machiavelli, the law of the west.* Might makes right. But is it moral?

The Pope says no, that preemptive war is aggressive war. Time counts in the violence play: you can answer but not precede. This line has always been part of the 'just war' concept. To some righteous or high moral horse mentalities it's a weasling technicality. We know who's good or bad. When George Bush sees signs and polls which say people consider him more dangerous than Saddam Hussein, that war is terror, he shall not be moved. He's righteous. He acts to save his people from another Saddam-fueled 9/11, to liberate the Iraqi people. Those Vietnamese villages which got burned to be liberated are not in his mind. He's thinking ahead. We'll rebuild and set them free. As the Tom Toles cartoon had it 'if you wait til he gets the irony you wait too long.'

Religion generally fuels the fire. St. Augustine argued that the purpose of war is peace, and that paradox or oxymoron or mythologisation of violence underlies most religious stances. Israel is bulldozing peace activists, Islam is issuing jihad calls, Christian Bush is leading the crusade. Give us time and we will remake the world in our beautiful image and new order – that's the promise. Give us time – a little irregularity/sacrifice/violence in the moment and then peace. The Hebrew preacher Ecclesiastes wrote that "that is why men's minds are full of evil and madness is in their minds while they live because their only future is to die." Obsessed with death, we do evil to try to exorcise death, limited evil to escape the ultimate evil which we cannot escape. We resign ourselves to violence and we rationalize and plunder it to feel alive.

There is no logic to the morality of violence. As the sixties protesters had it "fighting for peace is like fucking for virginity." There is no morality to violence. It's the defeat of morality, of a way to

8

live. The Pope is right on this one – war is always
a defeat for humanity

Blood Sacrifice

Most Americans don't do blood sacrifice, except for giving blood to the Red Cross. Most Americans don't kill goats or sheep or chickens ritually. If they drink the blood of Christ it's wine or grape juice. As we watch the reports of our fighting men making the ultimate sacrifice we don't see mangled bodies and blood, but faces of family pain and official piety. Mothers say he died doing what he loved in service of a cause he believed in. We change the blood into fine noble wine. The Secretary of Defense is already tipsy. Our now-dry President is in the grip of a mortal addiction.

A Day of Reckoning

Our leader promises 'a day of reckoning' for Saddam's regime – by which he means not just the shootout at OK Corral but a religious settling of accounts.

The ancient Egyptians reckoned judgment with a scale. Your heart in a canopic jar was weighed against a feather representing Maat – the goddess of justice and righteousness. Maat's consort Thoth, god of wisdom, recorded the verdict, and if you did not weigh righteously you got gobbled by Amet the crocodile god lying below the scales who was eager to eat the unworthy and deprive them of life. For well over four thousand years that image of scales and ultimate just reckoning has been alive in Egyptian culture. Tourists today buy 'the day of reckoning' on plaster plaques and painted papyrus. Scales of reckoning also appear on old Greek vases where Zeus weighs the fate of warriors and on Christian churches where Michael, god's warrior, weighs good and evil souls in judgment. Christians use both scales and the written record. In Michelangelo's Last Judgment in the Sistine Chapel there are two books – a big one of the damned and a smaller one of the saved.

The President's day of reckoning has a direct biblical echo in the book of *Daniel* which is set in 6th century b.c Babylon in the court of that Nebuchadnezzar whom Saddam openly emulates. Nebuchadnezzar in the Hebrew view is a vicious tyrant whom god humbles – making uum crawl on all fours with his hair and nails growing wildly like a beast's.

The Hebrew prophet Daniel interprets the king's dreams which foretell his inevitable downfall. His great image with head of gold, breast of silver, belly of brass, will be struck in its iron and clay feet by a stone (usually read as Israel) and his empire will topple. The great tree of his kingdom which fills the heavens will be cut down and left a stump. Nebuchadnezzar's son, Belshazzar, is also warned and punished. At a feast, Belshazzar drinks wine out of the gold and silver vessels his father had taken out of the temple in Jerusalem. A mysterious hand appears and writes on the wall '*Mene mene tekel u-pharsin* – God has numbered the days of your kingdom and brought it to an end; you have been weighed in the balance and found wanting.' Belshazzar quakes with fear. He is slain that very night.

Babylon is shocked and awed by God in both biblical apocalypses – Hebrew *Daniel* and Christian *Revelation (Apocalypse)*. The final reckoning is a cleansing bloody conflict which separates good and evil nations. Mighty Babylon's doom in the Christian *Apocalypse* will sound in a single hour and Jerusalem will triumph as the heavenly rich city with the tree and water of life.

The President of the most powerful nation on earth feels righteous attacking Baghdad. He intends to transform Babylon into liberated Christian Jerusalem. He's in charge of a resona... day of reckoning, confident that evil will be removed by good.
Is he God or Amet or another tyrant?

There will be more than one day of reckoning.

A Scene in Obscene War

CNN ran an elegaic piece April 5th called "The Road to Baghdad." Among other stories it included one of US soldiers in an Iraqi town surrounded by a crowd yelling angrily at them. The soldiers watched uneasily and uncomprehendingly. The voiceover said the soldiers had been invited by a religious leader, but the crowd hadn't known this and just vented anger or anguish at their presence. The soldiers' response was to kneel down and to turn their weapons upside down. This quelled and calmed everyone. It took my breath away and made me cry.

The line from Isaiah that we can beat our swords into plowshares and our spears into pruning hooks is inscribed on the wall of the United Nations. The text goes on to predict that man can come to not learn war any more.

Can war make peace as St. Augustine's "the purpose of war is peace" suggests? I presume the saint isn't cynical and just spinning or rationalizing. How could it be that fighting for peace isn't like fucking for virginity – i.e. the wrong tactic, as the Vietnam protesters chanted? Is war the required method to destroy a war-maker? Or is war the required pain that precedes the relief which comes when you stop banging your head against the wall? Or is it a mystery which can invoke its opposite – soldiers kneeling down and lowering their weapons? Christ and Gandhi and King preached peace and got assassinated as dangerous people. Everybody dies.

I search the news for bits of worry and self-consciousness – loving the soldier who fears his wife will think of him as a killer, applauding the officer who told the Marine to take down the American flag as we're not in Iraq to conquer but to liberate. In our wars pictures show soldiers fighting, suffering, and handing out candy to kids or sharing a smoke with a wounded enemy or carrying a wounded child. What you have to buy in a war scenario is that destruction is the necessary tool – like surgery. In this war we boast that we're even more surgical and precise in our targeting than in the 1991 Gulf War. We are destroying a regime of bad people not the good people they oppress.

We see fireworks more than rubble and body

parts. We see 24/7 coverage but we don't see much human damage or the dark side of destruction. "Iraqi Freedom" may seem less sanitized than the wars where no photo of wounded or dead was permitted, but it is really even more sanitized because it claims to show more. The generals warn us that war isn't pretty, that war is cruel, that we regret all casualties. But they and the networks are anxious to protect us from the real scene. The Greek dramatists too insisted violence occur 'off-scene' – which is the literal meaning of 'obscene.' Ted Koppel quoted a Jack Nicholson movie general who sneered 'you can't stand to see it' and Ted opined we could and promised he would show us.

Nobody admits to feasting on the drama – to loving the blood and guts and thrill of vicarious danger. Our media priests and political leaders perform rituals pretending objectivity, detachment, humanity, national piety. That beautiful moment on the road to Baghdad is not war but peace, packaged into the story of war.

Human history is a tragedy of ego and cruelty and lies. Only art approaches it. TV news is a soap – neither the real thing nor art, just entertainment.

Ends, Means, and the Present Tense

"The war in Iraq is really about peace" President Bush said on April 11, 2003. He and his regime confidently assert that the ends of peace and liberation justify the means of war and destruction.

It's an old trick question in ethics to ask if the ends justify the means. The trick is usually presented as checking out the ends. That is, a bad end doesn't justify any means, while of course a good end is just what justifies good means. As to bad means, you have to weigh the bad means (like war) against the good ends (like peace and liberation). And sometimes they are judged just, sometimes not. It's presented as a matter of proportion.

The devil is in the details of proportion of course. How many lives and wounds, how much pain, anguish and destruction should be sacrificed to

17

'peace and liberation?' Would we sacrifice bombing of our cities and destruction of our civilian population for the peace and liberation of Iraq as confidently as we sacrifice Iraqi lives and cities? How do we reckon costs of lives, cities, money?
Moral philosophers bicker. The Pope has condemned preemptive war as unjust and American neocon Catholic Michael Novak has hied to Rome to argue US righteousness.

Our ability to abstract and argue like this is often cited as our human genius. It's also clearly a curse. Life happens only in the present tense. Memory and imagination look back and forward and can make us ignore and rationalize the present, but morality happens only in the present and usually has a bodily not abstract character. We drop fire from the sky and wound, we do shoot or don't shoot. Making war and making peace are different: one accuses and rends, the other forgives and embraces. We're trying to do both at once and while that's clearly an improvement over a purely bellicose posture, it's also an illusion. In the present tense it's impossible. The Lieutenant Colonel who told his men to go down on one knee, turn their weapons muzzle down and smile, made peace in a scene of war. But mostly we've made war, bringing staggering military might against a defiant but ill-matched foe. We're Goliath here, not David.

Except we're an enlightened Goliath who really wants to be seen not as the giant but as the unarmored David, beloved entrepreneurial champion and chosen king of God.

TV coverage cracks and confuses our heads about time. What's going on, what's on tape, what's file footage, what's the story, fills the time. Very little is in real time except fireworks and reporters telling stories. It feeds our appetite for passing time, giving escape and intensity, but it's weak on the present tense – very much pushing off-scene (literally 'obscene') the broken bodies and buildings. President Bush announces he's upset by scenes showing carnage and looting. It's all really about peace to him, a future disembodied peace via a sanitized, not brutal, maiming, and ugly war.

When the finest collection of ancient culture was pillaged and destroyed in Baghdad the Bush regime comment was that it's terrible and untidy and the result of transition turbulence – i.e. not really our fault but the sad consequence of liberation from a brutal regime. Back to Saddam for blame, forward to liberation and fixing it. But whether 50,000 or 170,000 artifacts are gone or destroyed the cultural memory and art are savaged. Some reports already blame 'ignorant' Shia revenging their Sunni (Saddam) repression. Clearly the Baghdad Museum was not an asset equal to the oilfields for the American liberators. The looting is not just a transition in Rumsfeld's hypocritical shorthand, it is more war and ruin, bad means and no good end. When Rumsfeld was asked how we could have let this happen he reared mightily in his righteous fashion and snapped that we didn't let this happen. It happened, he said, no fault of ours, our men were probably protecting hospitals at the time. Already, he said, some people were returning things.

You can say that war is about peace but that doesn't make it so. That may be your desire for the future or your rationalization or delusion about the past. The only really moral mirror is the present tense – the first casualty of politicians always anxious to 'move forward' and 'get this behind us.' Whatever clever ends and means we construct, adduce, or asseverate, we act and will be judged in the present tense – the only place one can live or die.

Enemy Tactics

> "*An American soldier was wounded and Iraqis also by the enemy who fired a flare into an ammunition dump.*" CNN early summary of a huge explosion of ammunition in residential Baghdad, 26 April 2003

Who is the enemy? 'A person who hates another and wishes and tries to injure him – synonym: opponent.'

Am I George W. Bush's enemy because I oppose his war policies mounted in the name of freedom? I do oppose him though I do not wish to injure him personally. But I do wish and will try to 'take him out' politically. Is my desire murderous? Will the Secret Service check on me? How real and dangerous are words like 'enemy'?

In war the word 'enemy' licenses corporeal killing. You may, perhaps should, kill the enemy who by definition is one who hates you and

21

wishes to injure or kill you. A soldier's personal identity is effaced. He or she can't define the enemy or disagree with the leader. The job is to fight the enemy and that label 'enemy' makes violence become self-defense, as well as authorized by your country. The license to kill usually comes from religion (kill the infidels) or the state (kill terrorists or evil regimes). Private licenses to kill are discouraged. (You shouldn't kill members of ethnic or racial or gender groups you despise, or family members who irritate you, or most anybody else unless you have a very good and legally-defensible reason.) The enemy is the killable other. The US soldier who early in the Iraq War rolled grenades into his officers' tents violated the rules by changing enemies.

We often try to draw distinctions about killing in war. In Iraq we wanted to kill the most hostile soldiers – the Republican Guard and Fedayeen. We often let the regular conscripted army soldiers go if they would abandon their weapons and hostility and soldier status. We tried not to kill and maim children and innocent civilians but when we did we argued that it was a mistake or due to the brutality of warfare or the enemy's fault. The enemy, we said, lacked our scruples and deliberately imperiled civilians by placing armaments near them. We blamed the viciousness of the enemy who used innocents as human shields for their own hostilities. And, mostly, ultimately, we blamed the enemy because their evil provoked us to war.

When the ammunition dump exploded in residential Baghdad, the guarding American soldiers tried to help dig out the people buried in the rubble, and the crowd wouldn't let them. The Americans and the Iraqis couldn't speak each others' languages and there were no translators handy. So the soldiers couldn't argue that an Iraqi enemy had deliberately caused the violence, not the soldiers. In one bit of news footage an American soldier yells to his captain 'They don't understand' and the captain responds ' I know they don't understand. Neither do I.' The Iraqis are later reported to be saying that they had warned the soldiers to move the arsenal, that babies are buried alive.

The soldiers looked like an enemy; the angry crowd looked like an enemy too. Further violence was avoided because the soldiers withdrew. In many similar scenes soldiers sometimes shoot and crowds sometimes murder. Not just in Iraq but in Israel and elsewhere.

Could language have calmed this scene? With translators could soldiers and crowd have found a common enemy – an outsider enemy who wished to injure them both – whom they could blame and then work together to help the victims?

Violence can erupt on a word. Yell 'enemy' in war and people often die. Talk shows and politicians pontificate that Madonna and the Dixie Chicks and Hollywood figures aided the enemy in wartime by their opposition to our government's policy. The Congressional cafeteria in Washington serves 'freedom toast' and 'freedom fries' to verbally attack and eliminate the French for their words against our war.

This sense is not the children's rhyme that sticks and stones will break our bones but names will never hurt us. It's more 'them's fightin' words.' If words construct the enemy they're the beginning of war. How do we go from naming enemies – terrorist, tyrant, evil – to killing them? How do we move from opposition to attack? 'The time for talk is over,' Powell and Rumsfeld and Bush announced. 'The enemy means us harm and is moving secretly against us,' they said. 'We risk terrorist attack if we do not attack,' they warned. We go from words to war by ceasing talks and beginning bombing. We also go by abstraction – we don't kill men and women and children and cities but the enemy and evil regimes. We go by justifying our anger as self-protection and revenge. We go by collapsing present time into future intention: 'war is about peace.'

We go by defining and redefining words and staying on message – shutting down other language. We wage a war of words as well as of brute force. The US soldier who screamed at an angry Iraqi crowd "We're here for your fuckin' freedom" needed a translator. Americans have always been fond of the supreme court of the gun. In many a western, Law and Order and Education need force to protect them. Yet the words are what make the actions moral.

Words support ambivalence just as they construct it. An enemy today might have been a friend yesterday or become one tomorrow. Donald Rumsfeld met with Saddam Hussein twenty years ago and gave him weapons against Iran. Word language allows for another time, a different tense. It admits contradiction and paradox. Language can entertain the idea of loving your enemy, the idea of transcending or changing your definitions.

Language also allows conflict without physical killing. We can oppose verbally and not attack physically. We can articulate intense anger and refrain from bloody followup. We can make mental warfare and live to fight again and tell the tale. We can change our enemies and have new fights. In corporeal warfare we lose language and ambivalence. We cannot heal wounds of the flesh with words, or raise the dead.

That's what the children's rhyme means – the domains of sticks and stones and words are different. We try to teach children not to hit but to talk.

When the soldiers tried by sign language to signify that they weren't responsible for the carnage at the Baghdad arsenal they were not understood. When the crowd screamed the soldiers were murderers they were not understood either. Were they enemies?

President Bush is angry at Kofi Anan of the UN for calling the US the occupying force rather than the liberating force. President Bush is angry at world leaders calling the US unjust war mongers rather than freedom fighters. Presidents get angry and name their conflicts 'Just Cause' and 'Iraqi Freedom' not 'Kill the Bastards' or 'Smoke the Evil Ones.' They do this to distinguish brutal acts of the righteous from brutal acts of the evil. This is called rationalizing or spinning or lying or delusion. The acts are similar – bombing for example. Labeling alone changes the symmetry of the acts of 9/11 and the shock and awe bombing of Baghdad. We meant to inflict terror through the shock and awe of bombing brute force. We not only thrilled at our explosive might, we boasted we were the most stunning ...ilitary force in all human history. But we weren't monsters because we meant well and our motives were pure. We were good and the evil regime we swaggered to dazzle was not. They were brutal, cut out tongues, killed, gassed and impoverished their own people, swaggered and swilled scotch and had mistresses. We said we respected Islam, loved the Iraqi people, were bringing democratic freedoms. And we just had to make war because the evil ones wouldn't change any other way.

Most of the world has trouble with these distinctions. The real language that is being spoken is brute force. You can speak before you bomb and say you don't want to hurt anybody and you can speak after you bomb and say you're sorry if there were accidents. The bomb has a different language, one which does not support ambivalence or tense change. Americans don't face their own violence, not the deep psychological kind, not the obvious historical kind. When we railed about weapons of mass destruction, no one pointed out that like the crazy Shakespearean kings we're terrified of them because we've done the thing we fear. Americans don't look at the footage of Hiroshima and Nagasaki nuclear bombing, and Japan is no longer the enemy. Our myth is that violence is changed by good intentions, that it can be cleansing. Some will say it's a religious error, others that it's the sad Darwinian truth of survival.

Does it matter what we say? Osama bin Laden says he's a slave of God and is on a divine mission to revenge insult to Allah and his people. George Bush says he's on a divine mission to rid the world of evil. Both bomb. Do they differ? In enemy tactics, they are enemy twins – resorting to force, blaming their enemy, claiming righteousness, and wreaking savage damage.

Good Killing and Bad Killing

> *"I strongly condemn the killings and I urge and call upon all of the free world, nations which love peace, to not only condemn the killings, but to use every ounce of their power to prevent them from happening in the future."* President Bush, denouncing a suicide bomber attack in Jerusalem

President Bush criticized Israel on June 10th 2003 for attempting to assassinate a militant Palestinian Hamas leader, Abdel-Aziz al-Rantissi. The next day Bush criticized the answering Palestinian suicide bombing attack on a bus in Jerusalem. He urged 'free nations which love peace to not only condemn the killings but to use every ounce of their power to prevent them from happening in the future.'

What kind of power stops the killings?

There is killing power of course – the idea that

good killing can eliminate bad killing.

The President himself subscribes to this and he personally ordered the assassination killing solution for Saddam Hussein and his regime. Bush sent stunning military force against Iraq because he felt war was the good killing necessary to deal with 'evil.' Bad killing in his logic justifies good killing. Bush's administration presently defends the US preemptive attack on Iraq on the grounds of Saddam Hussein's brutality. Even if he didn't have weapons of mass destruction, the reasoning now goes, he killed and tortured viciously and therefore required killing. The agent's intention governs the morality in this reasoning. The 'free nations which love peace' kill righteously. The enslavers who love war kill wickedly. It's good guys and bad guys rather than actions that determine morality. This subverts classical ethics which says primary morality derives from the act itself, not from the intention or situation.

When Bush rebuked Israel for its attempted Hamas assassination, Israel claimed its own self-defense right to fight terrorist organizations and pointed out that the US had just taken this posture and action. The Palestinians argue the same claim – they say that Israeli occupation and military oppression are terrorism and that they too are only defending themselves and resisting evil. Good killing and bad killing become issues of point of view. Each position moralizes its hurt, revenge and righteousness.

The young Palestinian suicide bomber on the Jerusalem bus dressed as an Orthodox Jewish student. He disguised himself as one dedicated to the enemy religion. He is named a terrorist by those he fought against and a martyr by those he fought for.

Warriors & Martyrs

Was the suicide bomber a warrior or a martyr, or both, or neither? By conventional codes he's a guerilla warrior – disguising himself, sneaking in, sabotaging, not distinguishing the civilian and the military. That distinction between killable and non-killable is usually argued as an important element of proper warfare. Don't kill women and children and aged innocents, just combatants, soldiers garbed and properly identified as fighters. But these distinctions often dissolve even for us, the US, as the fire bombings of Dresden, the nuclear bombings of Hiroshima and Nagasaki, and the Vietnam and Iraqi wars demonstrate. War itself is clearly terrorism against civilian population as well as combat against deputed fighters.

The US press, like the Pentagon, tries very hard

in covering the Iraq war and occupation to emphasize the boundary between civilian and combatant – repeating the political refrain that we're only after Saddam and the hardliners, not against the Iraqi people. June 14th's *New York Times'* front page features a soldier comforting another crying soldier who is upset after seeing Iraqi children wounded when playing with ammunition. The sense is that soldiers are not cruel killing machines, rather that they care about Iraqi children. In fact they burned and maimed and orphaned and killed many Iraqi children. They just didn't mean to.

The suicide bomber meant to kill Israeli innocents. His terror is more malicious and unsentimental in intent. But the killing actions and the innocent dead don't differ. Does morality depend on the intention of the warriors?

When people vilified the 9/11 terrorists many said they were cowardly, by which they meant to strip them of warrior status. Just as we demonized the kamikaze pilots in World War II, we sought to deny the terrorists any sacrificial warrior role. The Al Qaeda discipline and courage and dedication were ignoble to us because destruction of us was their cause. We felt ourselves innocent, not the Great Satan of anti-Islamic oppression. So we resisted the idea not only that the terrorists were martyrs, but even that they were warriors.

We thought of our dead as martyrs because they got killed. One warrior/martyr distinction is about agency – active and passive. Warriors kill and martyrs get killed. Warriors seek the death of the enemy; martyrs suffer their own death as the enemy. Martyrs do not kill others. Those who choose martyrdom allow themselves to die for the sake of ideals and witness. The Palestinian bomber immolates himself like the Buddhist monks set on fire during the Vietnam War, personally for a cause, but his action is to kill others. The bomber is a warrior not a martyr. He kills. It's a useful distinction.

Being willing to die for your cause is necessary to martyrdom, but it's different from being willing to kill for your cause, which is warrior posture. Warriors are theoretically willing to die for their cause, but they try not to die. Martyrs endure others' violence and thereby reveal it and refuse it. They make peace by absorbing the violence and not returning it. Christ was not a warrior.

U.S. Warriors & Martyrs

One reason the US won world sympathy for the 9/11 attack was because those killed were seen as martyrs; they were killed for being in American buildings, sacrificed to an idea of war. President

Bush's response to 9/11 was to turn the savage brutality into full warrior response: kill the enemy. The bombing attack on Afghanistan was reprisal for terrorism, though the leader, Osama bin Laden, like Saddam Hussein, was not eliminated. Bin Laden had often assumed the martyr mode as justification for his war. He declared himself a slave of Allah and said he acted in reprisal for the evil done God's people and shrines. Saddam Hussein didn't strike a religious posture. He admired strongman Stalin and sought to be feared. Bush was betwixt and between: pious and martyred in justification, "smoking 'em out of their holes" strongman in execution. All three are warriors in action – ͻͻnding others to their deaths to execute their cause.

Jewish Warriors & Martyrs

Jews, until the founding of modern Israel, haven't been thought of primarily as warriors. To most Americans they have suffering biblical stereotypes, like their enslavement in Egypt in Exodus or the suffering servant of Yahweh and exile in Isaiah. The prophetic suffering servant figure is one who is innocent, who has done no violence nor had deceit on his tongue. Yet he is killed by those who vilify him, projecting their own violence and feeling righteous as they eliminate him as evil. The Christ story is modeled on this Isaiah figure. Modern Israel was achieved partly by guerilla warfare but also politically by Jewish martyr history. Most people take the cry 'never again' to mean 'this time we fight, no more Jewish holocausts.'

The great warriors like Joshua and David in Jewish tradition, are not the inspiration, the suffering victim history is. The legitimizing of Israeli violence similarly rests not on warrior history (we are great fighters) but on victim history (we are great victims). Israeli violence is cast by the Israeli government as only self-defense, exactly as US violence was rationalized by Bush – he said we needed to protect ourselves against another 9/11 massacre.

This is a clear pattern in legitimizing violence. We were injured, we will defend ourselves, preemptively or vengefully. Even legally we tend to excuse killing if we can persuade a jury that the killer thought he was acting in self-defense. Self-defense is much more primal and easier to understand than complicated history, land claims and numbers of killed.

Islam, which means the peace of surrender to God, is in popular American understanding a war religion – sanctifying holy war or *jihad*. President Bush thinks of the US and Israel as democratic 'peace-loving' nations and the Islamic terrorist menace looks like bad guys to him. Bush seems incapable of understanding US or Israeli violence except from the good guy point of view that legitimizes it.

Good killing doesn't eliminate bad killing. It echoes and promotes it. The power to stop killing is not adjectival and moralizing. As the old Hebrew adage goes "A bad peace is better than a good war."

Good killing and bad killing are enemy brothers, old stories like Cain and Abel, Ishmael and Isaac. You can tell who they are, not by their fathers who are the same, but by what they do. The murderer is the one who kills.

"Bring 'em on."

"Bring 'em on. We've got the force necessary..." President Bush, about Iraqi attacks on our soldiers, July 2, 2003

C'mon you fuckers
we'll kill you suckers

Blood and circuses
the emperor will be amused
the good ol' boy
never in combat
ace who combs his hair behind the plane
before you snap his prance
peppy, preppy, pious, pugilist
Gotcha

Bad Guy/Good Guy

"You help me find the bad guy or we come back with our tanks and run over your fields and break down your house."
American soldier to a northern Iraqi villager, July 17, 2003, CNN news

The soldiers face sniping resistance and are attempting to root out the fighters who blend into the Iraqi village population. So they're coercing information from the neighbors through the threat of ravage. This tactic is not exactly the same as the Israeli practice of destroying the land and homes of Palestinian suicide bombers' families. That is deliberately punitive revenge and it's also rationalized as deterrence. Our soldiers' tactic is simply brutal coercion, guerilla warfare, extortion.

Should 'good guys' get 'bad guys' by coercing and ravaging neutral guys? Didn't we disparage Saddam's inhumanity by pointing out that he terrorized his own people in a reign of fear and retribution? Or does war suppress humanitarian questions and radicalize everyone into good guys who are with us and bad guys who are against us? The soldiers who mistakenly kill civilians they think are hostile are excused because fear is seen as a reasonable excuse. Alan Dershowitz, sometime defender of civil rights, says even torture is allowable. Everybody knows people do these things. Warrior types sneer at liberal squeamishness. Ann Coulter swashbuckles that we should ravage and kill and convert the Muslims. As Yeats puts it "The best lack all conviction, while the worst / Are full of passionate intensity."

One reason it's so difficult to move from war to peace is that they're different tactics. War forces and peace frees. U.S. Americans love both force and freedom – the tough guys who triumph and the high ideal. As Tony Blair so deftly demonstrated speaking to the US Congress, we thrill to freedom talk, stand up and clap for it, are willing to die for it, love the flag for it. My favorite revolutionary war headstone reads "When I heard freedom was the cause my heart was enlisted."

But it's hard to love the soldier who says get me the bad guy or I ruin your fields and house. When Saddam Hussein terrorized and threatened his people and punished them for criticizing him we said he was a monster worthy of death. Is the soldier that, or does he get a pass because it's us against them and war is hell and any means possible is ok if it's a bad guy you're after?

The soldier is still in war mode, which is reasonable as he's being shot at. He's not a policeman or a peacemaker except in the war fantasy that killing and destroying will make all well in the end because we'll get rid of evil. Our exorcisms fail for several reasons, including the obvious trouble we have catching demons. Like Khaddafi and Osama bin Laden, Saddam Hussein, our Iraqi incarnation of evil, evaded our awesome decapitation campaign. This unnerves the Iraqis who are afraid he'll come back and it also punctures our apocalyptic pose. The day of reckoning George Bush promised Saddam Hussein is postponed due the sacrificial oblation's sneaking away to escape smiting. Death comes to us all in course, but taking out bad guys gives us the illusion that we're in charge and triumphal.

If we caught Saddam today and put his head on a pole as they did in 17th century Britain would all be well, would there be no more bad guys, would we be good guys because we killed the bad guy? The demons aren't only out there. It's a fantasy to think they can be packaged into regimes which can be changed like socks – the holy tossing the holey.

Is it a good guy tactic to destroy a person's field and home to force him to name his neighbor as a bad guy? Aren't these tactics we've deplored in other regimes? Are they good because we do them and we're good? What moral maelstrom do we descend to to delude ourselves so?

Most religious and moral teachings warn against thinking you're good. Call no man good is the counsel. The wisdom is that if you think you're good you're dangerous because you won't acknowledge where you're bad. Contrary to popular appetite it's not all or nothing, good or bad forever fixed, but separate actions in time. You can be good today and bad tomorrow, bad yesterday and good today. If you're free it's an open option.

The only unforgivable sin Christ named is confusing good and evil, calling evil good and good evil.

The bad guy doesn't define the good guy. Actions do.

Ruthlessness

> "*Dhuluaya, Iraq...US soldiers driving bulldozers, with jazz blaring from loudspeakers, have uprooted ancient groves of date palms as well as orange and lemon trees in central Iraq as part of a new policy of collective punishment of farmers who do not give information about guerrillas attacking US troops.*"
>
> Patrick Cockburn, *CounterPunch*, Oct. 14, 2003

Ruthlessness is conventionally condemned. To be without pity or mercy or feeling is thought cruel and inhuman. But in war the moral convention fades as men and women are licensed and charged to be ruthless. They must destroy and kill the enemy on behalf of their country which orders and sanctions it. In the *Bhagavad Gita* Krishna says the mode of war is apart from human time. A civil libertarian like Alan Dershowitz rationalizes ruthlessness and torture for the sake of one's tribe.

Normally we would reproach the punitive killing of trees and razing of homes. But the United States and Israel right now uproot ancient date palms and olive trees to coerce informing on kin and to punish families related to fighters. Ruthlessly destroying trees and homes is sanctioned as necessary action – to punish the family of an enemy and thereby deter bombing and encourage informing. The Romans sowed salt to punish the land and people they particularly despised. That long-lasting warrior brutality taught the same imperial lesson.

Stopping war is hard. At the end of *The Odyssey* Odysseus returns home and kills the suitors who have been eating at his house and stalking his queen. Odysseus and his son and father stand and fight gloriously to defend their property. When the hall is drenched in blood they prepare for an onslaught of vengeance which must follow. The families of the suitors will have to revenge their dead. Athena, goddess of wisdom and war and Odysseus' protector, asks Zeus to stop the fighting and he drops a pall of forgetfulness so that vengeance can fade. Even so Odysseus' own blood lust is up and he doesn't want to stop. Zeus has to hurl a thunderbolt at his feet to quell his fighting spirit. That works, and Athena in the guise of Mentor counsels

Odysseus to have a nice life. Humans without divine help tend to go on fighting in the Greek story.

In our recent war on Iraq, the Pentagon spent great energy praising the stunning power of our military prowess and the kinder gentler attitude of our troops. They weren't shouting kill kill kill. They were liberating, respecting Islam, loving the children. They weren't ruthless. The pictures showed men cry at the loss of comrades and the wounding of children. One soldier in Dhuluaya reportedly broke down and cried when bulldozing the fruit trees.

How do you turn from ruthless to compassionate? How change the actions from destruction to construction? If you haven't the power to make the conquered forget, nor the thunderbolt to check warrior passion, how does it happen? We tried proclamation. We announced that the time for shock and awe and forcing violence is over and we intend to make peace and rebuild civilization. But the way of force is not the way of freedom. Saying doesn't make it so. We started fighting because we abandoned words, spurned diplomacy, and said the time for talk was over. We speak the language of force and find it hard to translate into peace talk.

Getting back to words, making peace, beating

swords into plowshares and spears into pruning hooks takes mind, muscle, and a will to lose the weapons. It takes first the mastery of ruthlessness. We enter our own cloud of forgetfulness, ignore what we have done and do, call war peace and brutality liberation. The thunderbolts do not fall at our feet.

Evil Acts and Evil Actors

What is the difference between evil acts and evil actors? An act is an action, an actor an agent. Does evil come from acts or from agency? Both, you might say. Evil acts are evil and evil humans do evil acts. Can evil humans do good acts? Can evil acts do good? How do we regard and treat evil acts and evil humans? This is the question. How you answer here tells your tale, tolls the bell of your morality.

Bush & his war team believe evil acts can do good – as in bombing and destroying enemies and cities and orchards. This is acknowledged necessary evil which is justified (made good) by a good end. That end is to destroy perpetrators of evil acts, to eliminate evil humans – the doers of past evil acts and the future source and danger of more evil acts. The idea is if we get the source, we'll revenge and stop evil.

Recently we went after Saddam Hussein and

Osama binLaden who served as incarnations of evil men. One was a brutal dictator the other a terrorist who sought to destroy our nation calling it 'The Great Satan.' They ran countries and networks that hated us and wished us evil. So we bombed them and killed their supporters and killed and burned and wounded thousands of innocent people. Their deaths and wounds were regarded as collateral damage or tragic mistakes or fog of war errors; they weren't called evil acts because we did them meaning good. They were unfortunate sacrifices to our good action. Similarly our troops were the good agents of our necessarily evil acts in the service of our good ends. Their deaths and wounds and psychic trauma are called heroic, patriotic, noble. They are justified and ennobled by our good end – to eliminate evil.

The incarnations of evil in this case – Saddam and bin Laden – eluded our military prowess and continue to provoke and counsel evil. And if we do smoke them out of their holes – to use the President's favorite hunting figure – it's hard to imagine it will quell the evil feelings aroused by our 'evil-destroying' actions.

The sad truth is you can't stop evil acts except by condemning them and refusing to do them yourself. The dreamers who think if Hitler had been killed all would be well are foolish. Hitler made his evils legal, he passed laws. World leaders like Churchill thought he was good until it was clear how bad he was. Many went along. If soldiers like the Israeli 30 refused to kill, fewer people would be dead. Nazi is now code for evil but it comes from acts. There are many genocides – American Indians for example. Those who execute racist policies do those evil acts even if they have been victims in a former time of those acts. It is acts that define evil, not humans. Humans can be evil or good by doing evil or good acts. Acts don't have the human option. They are a better guide to good or evil.

Osama bin Laden and George W. Bush are both bent on destroying evil. They accuse each other of incarnating evil. They incarnate the weakness of a moral imagination that projects all bad onto an other and licenses murder. 'The Satan' in Hebrew means 'The Accuser.'

Wishing Death

*"I wish Wolfowitz had been killed. I wish all
the Americans here would be killed," said Ali
Hussein a grocer in downtown Baghdad. "The
Americans are not human beings. They are
monsters. They lied to the Iraqi people."*
New York Times October 26, 2003

I do not wish Wolfowitz had been killed, though
I consider him a war criminal, a reckless
belligerent and an evil actor in the US war on
Iraq. He was in the Hotel Rashid when a bold
attack rocked the luxury hotel with the tightest
security in Baghdad. Brigadier General Martin
Dempsey, commander of the First Armored
Division, told the Deputy Secretary not to take it
personally, but later before cameras an unshaven,
rumpled, wavering Wolfowitz tried to talk tough
but looked trembling and vulnerable. Hard not to
gloat that the armchair warrior got a slight breath
of the brutal whirlwind he kindled.

But killing isn't the answer. Everyone dies. We can glut our death wishes on the deep inevitable truth that no one escapes death – not the mighty, not the miserable, not the Deputy Secretary of Defense. The preacher of Ecclesiastes says that this is what makes men mad and puts evil in their minds – that their only future is to die. Religion wrestles with that very demon.

We wish death because we see the monster coming up on us.

When Ali Hussein the Baghdad grocer says Americans are not human beings, they are monsters and liars he's not just retaliating for ..vastation labeled liberation. He's echoing traditional figures for evil. The devil is a monster who eats us, hell is terrible maw, Satan is the great deceiver, the liar. Maybe the grocer just wants to feed people and make a decent life; maybe he's related to Saddam. He feels entitled to wish death on Paul Wolfowitz and all the Americans.

Paul Wolfowitz returns the wish – promising to destroy all who would attack us.

Wishing death is the problem. Resisting the monster is the cure.

Warriors & Liberators

"Our troops are warriors and liberators."
U.S. President George W. Bush, 11 November 2003

Warriors and liberators are not one. Forcing and freeing are different acts. The problem is time – you can't do war and freedom simultaneously. In Vietnam we burned villages to pacify them and it requires abstract thinking and wrenched words to recast that destruction as liberation. The soldier in Baghdad who yelled from his tank to hostile cries "we're here for your fucking freedom" voices the paradox. First I beat you, then I kiss you. It's not so much a perverse erotic routine as belief in a mysterious transforming power of violence.

The President's plan was to force in order to free. This is always the military rationale. We don't publicly pursue force for the sake of flexing mighty muscle, dominating, profiteering, or seizing resources. As Vergil's Anchises tells his son Aeneas in the Underworld, the destiny of great warriors is to rule for the sake of justice and order – "To pacify, to impose the rule of law/ To spare the conquered, battle down the proud." This formulation transforms war into a noble act, selfless and society-building. Blake translated that argument from the *Aeneid VI, 848* this way: "Let others study Art: Rome has somewhat better to do – namely War and Dominion."

When we say war is noble, well-meaning, self-sacrificing, does the power of words rule? Like transubstantiation, do the words change blood into bread? 'Hocus-pocus' is a deliberate corruption of "*Hic est corpus meum*" ("This is my body") – the words of Christian consecration making bread into the body of Christ. For the faithful, the words are sacred and transformative; for the faithless they are 'hocus-pocus,' a deception.

The President, high-priest of the nation, intones a consecration when he says 'warriors and liberators.' He builds on our "Battle Hymn of the Republic" which goes "As He died to make men holy, let us die to make men free." The model is skewed, however. Christ doesn't kill; he dies rather than kill. He is a liberator not a warrior. Hocus-pocus.

About the Author

Diane Christian is SUNY Distinguished Teaching Professor at University at Buffalo. She did her Ph.D. on William Blake at The Johns Hopkins University. She is the author of *Wide-Ons*, a book of poems, and, with Bruce Jackson, co-author of *Death Row* (Beacon 1980). She and Jackson directed and produced several documenta.y films, among them *Death Row* (1979), *Out of Order (1983)* and *Creeley* (1988). She is a frequent contributor to *Counter-Punch* and *Buffalo Report*, where, from December 2002 through November 2003, the material in this book first appeared.

About Urizen

The front cover image is from *The Book of Urizen*, William Blake's myth of primal fall from embodied life to abstraction. Urizen is primeval priest, sacrificer, spirit of righteousness – a very dangerous god.